Standing on the Deck of the *Titanic*

A Gay Catholic Looks at His Dysfunctional Church

By

Frank Oliva

To my dear friend Tom with much love and gratitude

Frank

An opinion from four years ago

This opinion is prompted by many causes. I will begin by telling a history of religion's place in my life and world view. It is integrally tied to my relationship to my father and to my sexuality. My primary purpose in stating this opinion is to present my religious confusion. I have rarely made a protracted statement such as this without first reaching a very painful point and that is very applicable today.

I was born into a very rigorous and observant Catholic family. ~~Though~~ my father's parents were as I would describe them, typical Italian Catholics, skeptical and somewhat peasant like in their observance. My grandfather was a typical male anti-clerical Italian Catholic, "church is for women," oddly enough his father had been a scrupulous observant Catholic. My Italian grandmother was that curious blend of superstition, devotion and the niece of a high cleric so her observance took another form. In spite of all this, once my father found the Jesuits in college he became an arch Catholic, much more devoted to his church and religion than the rest of his family.

My mother's side of the family was generally Irish Catholic devotional though my grandmother's father was born into a Sabbatarian Anglican family so there was some religious internal conflict. Nevertheless, my mother after 16 years of Catholic schools and a very devoted mother was typically Catholic. Both of my parents were very strict about their own attendance at Mass and felt very guilty if they missed a Sunday or Holy Day even if through no fault of their own.

Another thing that I think informed the faith on both sides of the family was the guilt, shame and stigma of illegitimacy. My Italian grandfather's mother had been the natural illegitimate daughter of an Austrian soldier. My Irish/English grandparents had married six months prior to the birth of their first child and had left San Francisco for the actual birth.

So when I was born the patterns were pretty much set. I attended Mass with my parents from infancy. The solemnity, sadness and lack of activity on Sundays began to bother me from early childhood. I liked the regularity and business of weekdays and the hustle, bustle and jocularity of Saturdays which also included my Grandmother Marjorie's joining us for Saturday dinner. But Sundays were boring, ruminative and eventually opportunities for childish sex play which passed into guilt, shame, embarrassment and discomfort. I did not like the idleness of Sundays and it made me feel sad and morose.

Once I had been caught and shamed by my father for childish masturbation, the conflict of Sundays became almost unbearable. I was three years old when he shamed me. This would become my main cross in life. How such pleasure could lead to such agony was completely beyond my understanding.

In 1958, a month before the election of John XXIII, I started first grade at St. Brendan's, a very upwardly mobile, upscale, middle class parish in San Francisco. Adrian Dominican Sisters taught there and I idolized my teachers. I wanted to please them. I wanted to do well. I wanted to be right. And I saw that through them and the church I could find a way to hide my shame over the masturbation conflict by identifying myself as a prospective seminarian, and eventually priest. This pleased my father who was still obsessed with my sly masturbatory activity. When time came to make my first confession, before my April 1960 First Communion, I agonized over how I would finesse my continual masturbatory compulsion. I resolved on the jesuitical identification of disobedience for masturbation and when I masturbated, which I enjoyed immensely up until the dry orgasm, after which I was overwhelmed with guilt and shame and hated myself. I would carry this guilt about the lies in Confession well into adulthood.

Nevertheless, things got to the point where I would look at my First Communion photo as the good Mark and when I would masturbate, which was often, as the bad Mark. This conflict became inextricably enmeshed with my religious beliefs. I became very well versed in the intricacies of the Catholic Faith, never questioning any of its teachings, and became very familiar with faith, dogma and ritual. I loved the trappings, the vestments and the ritual. I became obsessed about little things like the altar of repose and mesmerized watching Sr. Emile Marie encrusting the cross with gold tin-foil for Holy Week. When I reached sixth grade and was trained as an altar boy I had also reached the point where my orgasms became much more intense and very messy. Nevertheless I became the very best and most reliable altar boy and Monsignor's favorite. I reveled in being Altar Boy number one, it gave me status as well as thinking it might please my father, who I felt despised me because I was such a poor athlete and a continual masturbator.

From this point things just got more intense, conflicted and reached a point where I hated to be alone with my father. I was so afraid he would begin questioning me about my incessant masturbation. I tried to be perfect in school and in service activities. I persisted in claiming I was heading for the priesthood. At this point I was the most rigid Catholic, simply tortured by the guilt and shame but also the pleasure my sexual activity brought me.

I had also discovered how intense my erections were when I looked at the male pornography which I found in drugstores and the back of magazines like *Esquire*. Eventually I mailed away for a catalog of very hot men's underwear. This stuff got me even more intense orgasms and eventually, when my father discovered that I had been receiving it regularly in the mail, it seriously upset him and increased his concern for me, and served as a great occasion for more dishonesty.

In my senior year of high school I was completely scandalized when we were on retreat and a young priest celebrated an intimate Mass without proper vestments. It upset me so much I could barely stay in attendance.

After high school graduation I went to Santa Clara and was now in the company of my idolized Jesuits. I think the idolization had a subliminal eroticism. I did not want to have sex with these men but there was nething strange about my obsession. ould they bring me the longed for stitution of my value as a human being? Would they solve my sexual crisis? But it seemed that things just got crazier and crazier and I got more and more schizophrenic. My Catholic rigidity seemed to match my sexual activity which from April 1971 now included furtive cruising and orgasmic activity with other men. One telling incident at Santa Clara was when I walked out of a lecture by Hans Kung as he spoke about the ordination of women. I was so scandalized and conflicted I demonstrably exited my seat and the church. The more I engaged in secret sex with men,the more rigid I became in my dogmatic beliefs and the more conflicted I became. I tried to be perfect in my beliefs and observance in order to hide my shame over what I was really doing. I never questioned any pronouncements or scriptures though I was definitely moving into thought processes that were less than orthodox.

Despite my out of control sexual behavior I decided to proceed dishonestly with the "vocation" which I thought would solve my conflicts, make me acceptable to my father and give me a secure life. I entered the Jesuits on August 17, 1974 filled with trepidation but with hope that I would be able to finesse this dilemma as I had done with the tortured logic of my first confession. But I had read enough to know that a day of reckoning was approaching with the Long Retreat. Still, ever the perfectionist, I thought I could prove my worth by doing everything by the book. From the beginning there were signs that I was in the wrong place. On the first day I was suffering from a bad cold. As the days went on my uneasiness increased. I tried to fit in, be one of the guys but I was so brittle, fragile and uncomfortable. After the second year novices had taken their vows and I was designated Music Rex and Sacristan. I had the false security that everything

11

was going to be OK. Next came collar day, what used to be cassock day. I was so sick during the "Collar Day" Mass that I had to spend most of the consecration in the sacristy. Life continued for about a month before "Grape Season" somewhat uneventfully on the outside. (Parenthetically, in the California Province of the Jesuits, the growing and harvesting of grapes to produce a very widely used altar wine allowed the participation of the novices in the harvesting of the grapes.) On the inside I was fighting my increasing horniness and the fear I had brought with me into the Novitiate.

Around October 1st we drove in caravans from Santa Barbara to Los Gatos for Grape Season. In some ways it was like a vacation, a fun time. Los Gatos however only made things worse. I saw hot guys in Los Gatos and I craved them. I wanted to make this Jesuit thing work but I could see that I was definitely approaching a crisis. As we returned to Santa Barbara days before Halloween and also Long Retreat, which was set to begin on November 6th, I was filled with doubt dread and fear. I knew I would have to confront my BIG LIE when the time came for the General Confession. On the morning of the third day of Long Retreat I knew I had to get out of the Novitiate but I was deathly afraid of the consequences and repercussions. Just before lunch I had made my decision, I would run away and strike out on my own. Like all novices I had no cash or credit cards. I did not know where I was going. I was so afraid of facing my parents and having to explain why I could not stay in the Jesuits. I packed my duffle bag with socks, underwear, my cross and shaving stuff, then went across the valley to the Manor House to write a letter to the Master of Novices. I told him, in the letter that I could no longer live a lie, that I needed the month of Long Retreat to figure out what I was going to do, and I asked him not to tell my parents of my departure. I then masturbated for the first time since I had entered the Novitiate. That was incredible.

I returned to my room with my clip board and simply waited for evening curfew when everyone else would go back to his room. Dinner in silence that night was very difficult. I was saying Goodbye to the one thing I thought would make everything all right in my life. After the final colloquy from the Master that night, while everyone else returned to his room, I retrieved the bag I had stashed in a ravine and headed out the gates and down the road to Highway 101, put my thumb out and hitch hiked to Los Angeles. It turned out the guy who stopped for me was a Gay man heading to the baths on Melrose Avenue in West Hollywood. He wasn't interested in me but he was willing to take me and pay my admission to the baths.

From this point I headed in stages to New Orleans and had a lot of sex on the way. I did have one very powerful experience of being completely in God's hands when I was hitchhiking in Norman, Oklahoma. I felt menaced by a man who had picked me up. I asked to get out of the car and found my self [one word?] on a very shaky bridge which rumbled and shook when the Semi-trucks passed me. It was dark, the sky was very clear and I had a deep sense of being completely in God's hands despite my extremely negative view of myself and my abject failure and sinfulness.

I continued to try to reconcile my sexuality with my religion. While I worked in New Orleans I was sexually active and I was a regular attendee at Mass.

In early December I received a telegram from my parents. I was dismayed that they had found me. I wanted to be the one who communicated with them. After Christmas, when my father told me that there might be a place for me at my old high school I decided to return to California. I decided I would try this new avenue. For some reason I also contemplated returning to religious life. It still seemed like the best option to find security. I had some really great experiences while teaching at Newman. I made a really beneficial friendship with Dennis. Unfortunately I also returned to the closet from which I thought I had escaped.

During my time at Newman, my religious and sex life were as conflicted as ever. There were parts of teaching which I loved and parts that I hated and I think much was tied up in my conflict over my perfectionist ideas and the disconnect with what I was doing. I wanted my students to be perfect while I was absolutely anything but perfect. I became obsessively moralistic about cheating and drug use and incredibly judgmental about my brother and his emerging sex life while finding my own hauntingly unacceptable. My judgments about others severely affected my relationships, all the time I was sneaking around bathrooms, beaches, and bath houses and bars and trying to reconcile my behavior with my extremely orthodox religious views. I had not begun to question any parts of the bible with the exception of the writings on homosexuality. I believed in evolution but felt it could be reconciled with the bible. All of the stories about Christ and Mary remained unquestioned.

After three and one-half years of teaching and a summer with SRT with much sexual acting out, I decided to apply to graduate school and pursue a career in the theatre. My sexual behavior was becoming much riskier and yet when I would come back to my apartment after a night of cruising I would find myself falling in front of the cross crying, begging for this behavior to stop.

The summer before graduate school I spent in San Francisco at ACT. The first five weeks were chaotic with a whole lot of sex culminating in my contraction of hepatitis and probably AIDS. I was back home to watch the funeral of Paul VI and election of John Paul I, and at the same time I was plotting my living situation in Irvine as a sexual companion to an older gentleman who would pay my room and board. I had already taken money for a blow job in Golden Gate Park so I was having few qualms about being remunerated for sex with room and board.

Once at UCI I realized very quickly that the sex for room and board was not going to work but I did not seek other arrangements until the second quarter. That is when things got really crazy. I moved into a share apartment and decided I would become a paid

Advocate hustler, sometimes even with my roommate at home. This perhaps sent me to the most depressing depths emotionally I had ever experienced. I became ruled by the telephone and the creepy "Johns" with whom I had to provide sexual companionship. At the same time I tried to go to Mass. I felt horrible on Easter Sunday 1979 during the Newman Center Mass. Yet I continued to exploit any opportunity for sex and money.

During the summer of 1979 I had the opportunity to intern as a Stage Manager at Santa Clara University and during one of my off hours, while cruising a public restroom I was arrested and arraigned. My life had really reached a state of incredible depravity. Still I continued to try and hustle as I had at UCI. When I was let off with a fine I was so relieved I thought I was going to change my ways, but I didn't.

I had however stopped hustling at least in the newspaper. I still was trying to reconcile my compulsive sexual habits with my very orthodox religious practice.

During my second year at UCI my sex and my religion were a little less conflicted than the previous year. I did have one very interesting eye opening discussion with a fellow student who was also an Evangelical pastor. He basically said to me that I couldn't just pick and choose what I wanted and didn't want from the Bible. It gave me pause but I continued to do just that. It did however start me looking at my personal belief system; I was much more content with the religious practices in which I was engaging. I had a much better Easter than I had the year before.

When I graduated I took another one of my extended sex vacations to wend my way to Santa Rosa and then on to my job at San Francisco Opera. After just two years I was back enmeshed again in the behavior which had gotten me hepatitis and AIDS. Even though I lived between St. Philip's and MHR parishes I decided to attend the Cathedral because it was close to the Opera House, my place of employment. At that point I had squirreled away the comments of my Evangelical friend. Sometimes I was troubled by the homilies which I found excessively homophobic but since many things about my sex life, hidden from my parents, were homophobic I guess I shouldn't have been surprised.

On the weekend before Thanksgiving when I was trying to date a man in whom I had lost sexual interest shortly after the first date, I went to Dignity with him. It was an amazing experience. I finally felt really comfortable at church but eventually would use the coffee hour as a place to meet tricks.

Dignity made a big difference in my life and my self image. It opened a world that would give me a break from theological debate until I entered recovery. But the battle between sex and religion was heading for a big crisis not to mention the big deal about still being in the closet to my parents.

I continued to have miserable results in my search for a sex partner who could also be a life partner. This was largely the result of my loss of interest of a sex partner as soon as the sex lost its edge. My sex life got a lot worse and the compulsive nature of it just continued to get worse and worse. Meanwhile I became so conflicted about my sex life and my religious beliefs that I was seriously coming unglued.

There was a three month period which I spent in Europe at the beginning of 1982. My life was essentially the same, lots of sex yet continuing to attend Mass. I returned to San Francisco to the worst recession I'd seen up until the most recent. I was at a very low point financially, but I did return to Dignity and my sex life was pretty much the same. I organized the first Dignity Pilgrimage and returned to my Jesuit fantasy. I did not have many beefs with the Church or Bible. I just wanted to be able to accept myself and have the Church accept me and my friends. In May of 1982 I had sex with an anonymous window cruiser and contracted herpes from him. It was in the early days of the AIDS crisis and I was convinced that this was my first AIDS infection and initial contact. It was eventually diagnosed but I could not afford the medicine. Although I had been somewhat frightened when I got hepatitis this was the first really significant AIDS scare.

In June I made a trip to San Diego and on the way experienced a mental and spiritual crisis. At my friend Tim's house in Laguna Beach, I talked to a priest on leave-of-absence about this spiritual crisis and wanted to have him hear my confession. He said he did not have faculties so while in San Diego I tried to contact a Jesuit I had known at Bellarmine College Prep when I was a senior in college. I told the priest who heard my confession my whole story and he was very concerned, sympathetic and forgiving. He sent me to a Jesuit therapist in San Francisco. It was a very kind and comforting gesture and ultimately beneficial. It was through the San Francisco therapist, Curtis that I found a recovery program, since I had been seeking spiritual help through the Sacrament of Confession, but when I think about it today did it really make sense to send me to a celibate Catholic priest to deal with my conflict over sexuality and spirituality? As I think further about it today I think it actually contributed to rekindling my Jesuit fantasy and enticed me with the hope of satisfying my father and hiding my homosexuality.

And so began my rapid decline to the bottom that would bring me into recovery. Curtis could not help but recognize the obsessive compulsive person he saw reflected by my insane behavior. He was in recovery himself, but he did not identify himself at the beginning. As he listened to me it wasn't long before he presented me with the first three steps of recovery. I said I thought they were great but I did not see my need for them. When I drank I definitely drank alcoholically but my sexual compulsion masked my ability to recognize my alcoholism. So as I spiraled down to my bottom my awareness of what was happening to me was heightened significantly. Three things that became eminently clear were that until I came out to my parents my torture was going to continue, until I became self supporting through my own contributions there was going to be little progress and my life was going to have to experience a radical change.

Meanwhile my sex compulsion and my religious rigidity were doubling exponentially. At this point my religious doubts had not begun to press on me.

In March 1983 I finally hit bottom. Curtis gave me an ultimatum that I had to start attending recovery meetings. I was so afraid of going that this was the only way to get me into some kind of recovery. At first I was very skeptical about my own alcoholism but as I began to attend meetings I became more aware and convinced that I was in the right place. My willingness to believe that God really was in control was revealed very early, around the third day of attendance at a recovery program. In spite of my very empty pocket book I decided to have my dirty clothes washed at a fluff and fold. On my way to the neighborhood site I was literally stopped in my tracks by a "power greater than myself"; I had to turn around and go to a Laundromat where I would have to do my own laundry. It was the first sign that my life was really changing. I was still as bigoted, self centered and confident that I was always right as I had ever been, but the friends I was making in AA were showing me a different path and convincing me that I really am an alcoholic, that I could feel I had found a different path and that my life was changing.

This huge event was only the beginning. It did have some significant impact on my religious beliefs. At first one of the biggest changes was that I stopped looking at God as a servant whose job was simply to perform whatever task I presented Him to do. I began to realize the incredible arrogance of my stance. I still hadn't fully embraced the principles behind the 11th step; I was still making very specific requests convinced that I was right about everything that was important to me. At this time however there were a number of gigantic hot potatoes between the Gay community and the Catholic Church and one of the biggest was Archbishop John Quinn's recommendation about *Ministry to Catholic Homosexuals*. One of the most hypocritical pronouncements ever promulgated, it really raised the ire of Dignity (an organization of Gay Catholics) and by association, of myself. At the same time Dignity was moving toward opening negotiations with Holy Redeemer to make MHR its home base. Up to this time MHR had been a moribund parish where Fr. Tony Maguire had been sent to close it down. But as the AIDS crisis prompted the return of many fallen away Gay Catholics there was a revitalization happening at MHR with or without Dignity. I think Tony was frightened by the anti-Papal stances of Dignity and he did not want them muddying his waters. He was somewhat ambivalent about the nature of his Gay parishioners and he was occasionally condescending, however he did arrange a meal whereby a number of us actually sat down to dinner and conversation with the Archbishop. It was a start but there was a long way to go.

At that point I still carried enough sexual guilt that I wanted the Pope to make me alright and when he spoke in the opposite direction he inflamed me to the point where I would call up prominent Catholic priests to tell them in no uncertain terms how I felt about the Pope and his pronouncements. I really was afraid of him, however but I was still not accepting myself.

During that first year of sobriety I actually entertained the thought of re-applying and re-entering the Jesuits. I had become so religiously pious and rigid, I figured that they would welcome me back with open arms. When it became clear that I was not going to be welcomed back I was very disappointed. Three months after that essentially unspoken rejection, having become so dangerously rigid that I snapped and one night in July I decided to return to cruising Collingwood Park. It was disappointing and ultimately unsatisfying but it did begin to change my puritanical outlook on sex. Gradually I returned to many different sexual venues and did reach a point where I really craved a relationship with a man with whom I could fall in love.

While all these things were going on I was beginning to have doubts about some things in my religion but I was certainly not admitting them. In fact my rigidity was becoming worse and my expectations of every one else conforming to my way of thinking were becoming more divisive, actually separating me from many. As I look back on this I can see how much this part of my shame-based self, using the obligation to be right as a way of hiding my shame. Instead of owning this disowned part, how much was I forcing myself to be right in anything I held true especially in my Catholic faith. While I was fighting and protesting hierarchical decisions I was behaving in the same way myself.

Once I became involved with Steve I found that it was very hard to be faithful. The old problem of getting bored with the familiar and always seeking the dangerous and the adventurous is something with which I have had to contend all my life.

Another thing that was becoming apparent was that in spite of my rigidity with regard to religion I still did not have a very good relationship with God. Since I was so absolute and judgmental of others it is not surprising that I should have fashioned a punishing and unforgiving God in my own image. While this was the norm with the same kind of lack of forgiveness, that I had reached a point of intolerability when I was finally diagnosed with pneumocystis pneumonia in October of 1993. In those days such a diagnosis was an almost immediate death sentence and hence I was filled with fear. In my fear I sought counseling with Sr. Teresa at MHR and in the course of the counseling she recognized how miserable my relationship with God was and how terribly fear based my entire spirituality was. She suggested I turn to what she called "the Grandma God." Because my maternal grandmother had been such an unconditionally loving presence in my life I was very grateful for thinking about God as loving me like my grandmother had loved me. This helped me a lot. After three episodes of pneumocystis with the accompanying pentamidine, Sr. Teresa commented in spring 1994 that I had stopped dying of AIDS and started living with it. In May 1994 I was diagnosed with diabetes and this infuriated me. It also spurred me into lots of physical exercise and I started to do a lot better. Meanwhile my T-cells were sliding and I started to be followed for CMV retinitis, the next expected Opportunistic Infection. 1995 involved lots of travelling and lots of concern about CMV retinitis and psychological problems and anger. During this time our dog Wolfgang was suffering more and more seizures and other health problems. But he brought me my next important religious God-experience. Following one of his many seizures, which used to upset Steve so much, I was granted the insight that no matter what Wolfgang did I would never stop loving him. Likewise I came to believe that no matter what I did or had done that God would not stop loving me. Like the Grandma God awakening this was a very important awakening. Unfortunately during this time I was having a lot of difficulties with gender neutral references to God at MHR and at meetings and discovered how this was another area where I wanted to exert my shame based driven control.

As our 1995 year of constant travel came to a close I experienced a severe emotional melt down after we had spent a weekend in Palm Springs. I really became aware of how much Steve was not interested in me sexually and this was devastating for me. Still we celebrated our ten year anniversary on December 28th and headed into one of the most difficult years of my life, 1996. My CMV had reached a very dangerous point and I was cruising down to 95 pounds as my diarrhea was incessant. I was having up to 20 bowel movements a day. After refusing to try any antiretroviral medicines since my congestive heart failure in 1993, I decided to give one a try. It did nothing and by September I was in the hospital on morphine. I think I was released to go home and die. I became a hospice patient in November and just continued to slide. In January of 1997 another pneumonia episode looked like my last. By the first of February I had given up any hope of getting better. I told Steve I was going to stop all medications since none were working. My hospice nurse asked for one more week and I consented reluctantly. That week Steve found a digestive enzyme which seemed to be working. In June we got a rescue Golden to replace Wolfgang who had died in March of 1996. I graduated from Hospice and Steve took me to Italy.

Financially those were very rough times. Steve had gone on Family Medical Leave to care for me while I was under hospice care. In January 1998 I started a new AIDS medication cocktail and things started to get so much better that I thought I could return to school and start a new career. This was stopped after one month when I developed another case of pneumocystis. About the same time I had been hit by an unexpected financial crisis. I had gone from indebtedness of $500 in July 1994 to $26,000 in August 1999 due to the distribution of my 401K which resulted in the taxability of my Social Security, something for which I had not planned.

All through this time I had been reading assiduously every day and some of that reading had been religious and biblical. Somewhere during the early 2000s I started having questions about my beliefs. When I was trying to be perfect or to hide my shame by acting like I was perfect and insisting on being right, I rigidly held to whatever I had been told to believe or made me look right, at least in my eyes. As the stance of the church became all the more hostile toward Gay persons, all the time covering up pedophile scandals, I got angrier and more questioning.

My closer reading of scripture and other commentaries contributed to my questioning. Biblical descriptions of the cosmos, the location of heaven and things that were completely contradictory to reality began to bug me. Since I had always loved things like Christmas and the Saints and other pious stuff I really became like a child discovering that Santa Claus was really one's parents. I was very disappointed. I tried to seek help in these areas with priests but they were of little or no help. Then I began to question the very basis of belief. I began to have trouble with the Creed. I was disturbed by the inconsistency between one Gospel account and another. The more I read the more discouraged I became. I began to see large holes in the fabric. Whether it was those beliefs which were not even based on the bible or the unlikely stories of Jesus being absolutely alone with the woman at the well, or the unwitnessed temptation in the desert, my feelings were how could any one have known about these unless he was recounting them himself. Then reading works about finding the historical realities of the time were throwing more confusion at me.

Once we had moved to Oakland and the new AIDS cocktail had started to return some regularity to my life I became much more immersed in sponsorship. Newer guys asked me to be their sponsor, not the other way around. They had and have been a very special gift. They have also helped me to approach religion and spirituality from a very different outlook, particularly respecting belief systems other than my own, and then causing me to subsequently question my own. I am not sure where the drift began but some of the issues revolved around the exposure of the hypocrisy of the church hierarchy with regard to accepting open homosexuals versus the cover up of the pedophile scandal. Once Ratzinger was elected as Benedict XVI and his destruction of the church was formalized as a papacy hell bent on eliminating those who did not agree with him, my cynicism became extreme (as in how could any Holy Spirit be involved in choosing such a venal and vile candidate, let alone persons like Rodrigo Borgia).

As this more questioning attitude grew so did my discomfort with the conflicts appearing in scripture. I had identified long ago my dissatisfaction with the treatment of Gays within the church and the confusion around actively homosexual priests. My first response had been anger, disgust and jealousy. Oddly enough I gradually became more accepting of imperfect or simply human "human" behavior of men trapped in a world from which they could not extricate themselves. I also started to see how the simple basic message of Jesus had been corrupted by the drives of self-interest, control and shame.

As much as I had wanted to be a celibate clergyman, I began to see how much this had been tied up with my desire to escape from the self I was not accepting. One of the big events on this journey involved a series of Fourth

Steps and counseling with men like Jack Fertig, who encouraged me to look at my relationships with Father, Church, Authority and God. This had grown out of a Fourth Step regarding anger centered in my reaction to my scolding mother and by implication any scolding or disapproving woman. From this has grown the doubt about participating in a church which seems so hypocritically disapproving of me and those who are like me.

Next comes the seemingly irrational embroidery around the person of Jesus. Was it simply to make his message more cogent that all the trappings of Divinity such as Virgin Birth, a visit from the Three Kings, Transfiguration etc., were added to this simple carpenter's son story who had the insight that God loves us because he created us and that he simply doesn't want us to hurt ourselves or others? Was the Nicene Creed formulated as a political settlement rather than an actual statement of belief? Was the need to make Jesus a son of God something like Augustus' elevation to the same position, a placement which makes others respect him more? How does any of this fit in the vastness of the Universe? Do Jesus' denials during his time on earth, which are recorded clearly in the Gospels, point to some other answer? Are the conflicts among the various Gospels simply examples of the crises in which each of the evangelist's communities were suffering? What does "the Kingdom of God is at hand" mean? Is it simply an internal transformation not an actual power shift?

I think I have reached the point where this inventory has become redundant. What occurs to me is that the comment of my Evangelical friend at UCI ~~that~~ keeps resounding in my head, once I begin to question one portion of scripture I end up questioning many if not all those things I find either unbelievable or unacceptable. I find

myself in a great quandary and seek
help as I have so many other times.

My Present Views

When I wrote the previous article, I was in the middle of my Second Saturn Return. As you probably know, a year is the time it takes for our planet to revolve around the Sun, just as a day is the time it takes for our Earth to make a single rotation on its axis. This is also true for the other planets. The planets closer to the Sun have years shorter than ours. The planets beyond the Earth in relation to the Sun have years that are longer. The planet Saturn has a year that lasts 29.45 Earth years. There is a wild card in the whole Astrological System designed by the Egyptian Ptolemy and Ptolemy postulated a geocentric universe, which it isn't. This wild card has an even more confusing aspect which is that in this system the planets actually appear to reverse direction. In Astrology each planet is expected to have a positive and a negative influence based on its position at the time of each person's birth. Now the role of Saturn is educative and disciplinary. Therefore, by astrologers, the Second Saturn Return is regarded as a pretty big deal and those issues that were bothering individuals during the First Saturn Return as the individuals are nearing the age of thirty but were not resolved, return to plague this individual as he or she approaches age fifty-nine. Well, when I wrote the previous preceding statement I was in the middle of my Second Saturn Return and that was only one aspect of my unresolved issues.

Now I want to address my issues around the Catholic Church with more reason and less hysteria. I will try to take these in a logical sequence. I will begin with a cosmological view of how Scripture and the Church evolved and then determine which parts of these things apply to me and then how we all fit in the scheme of world history and religion, and finally, how the Catholic Church has failed me and so many other Catholics.

The Scriptures that Preceded Jesus and the Gospels that Followed

According to Hebrew and Christian tradition, God created the world, basically the universe in five days and then He filled the earth with animals and finally on the evening of the sixth day He created Adam and Eve. He created them in the so-called Garden of Eden in the Fertile Crescent at the juncture of the Tigris and Euphrates River not far from current Baghdad, Iraq. Now, some Christian scholars have tried to construe the "six" days of creation as a symbol for the millennia that it actually took according to the geologic record. They have even tried to reconcile the Genesis creation story with the evolutionary theories of Charles Darwin. For those who adhere to a literal reading of the Bible this is almost, if not indeed, impossible. But the first thing we should remember is that the book of Genesis was written even after Moses, though he is credited with authorship. And several millennia passed before Moses even lived. In fact the first books of the Bible are actually compendiums of many other cultures' cogitations about the universe, creation and mankind.

In his excellent book, *Who wrote the Bible*, UC Berkeley professor, Richard Friedman, makes the point that there are many reasons to doubt that Moses wrote the *Torah*, the first five books of the Bible, because among other things he describes his own death and then claims that he is the most humble man who has ever lived, an unlikely claim for a man who is truly humble.

Some scholars believe the first books of the Bible were written after the Babylonian captivity by the same writer who wrote the book of Esdras. Even the Dead Sea Scrolls don't bring the mystery to an end. Obviously, the stories were part of an oral tradition until scribes could record them in some sort of readable format. But it is amazing how much of an oral tradition can survive until the scribes can scribe it.

All of this is by way of saying that we really don't know who was responsible for recording everything we have learned from ancient sources. One thing is for sure, Adam and Eve were not keeping a diary. Even the beginning of Genesis has been shown to be from separate sources, one that uses the name Yahweh or Jehovah for God and another uses the word Elohim translated God or Lord. The book of Deuteronomy is considered to be by a completely separate author.

Then there is the issue of interpolating stories outside the Israelite community such as the story of Noah and the flood, which has been identified as a Babylonian myth which one could use as evidence for at least some of the Old Testament being written after the Jewish Babylonian Captivity.

The next set of questions is about the veracity of the New Testament. The first writings about Jesus after his death and resurrection are *The Passion Narrative, The Sayings Gospel* and *the Q Document* which have been considered as the original sources for what are known as the similar yet different so-called Synoptic Gospels, *new sentence* from a Greek word meaning taken all together, as the Gospels of Matthew, Mark and Luke tell the story of Jesus in a similar manner and order, unlike John's Gospel which takes events in a different order and leaves out many shared stories in the Synoptic Gospels. While the Synoptic Gospels are grouped together because they each try to tell stories in a chronological order, only Matthew and Luke differ with regard to the infancy stories details. Meanwhile, the principle differences between Mark and Matthew's presentation concerns the conflict between Christ's adherents and the larger Jewish community and the deepening divide that had festered between the time of composition of the earlier and the later.

Luke takes a much more Biblical approach. He strives through his fictitious creations to make Jesus the obvious successor of the whole of Jewish history doing things like having three unlikely foreigners visit him in a manger. And he presents him as related to John the Baptist who has parents who are his mother's relatives. He creates a genealogy through his father's heritage despite the premise that he had had nothing to do with his birth. But his desperate attempt is to link Jesus with the royal tradition of Israel.

The Gospel of John is so different from the other three that it even begs the question of how someone who was even a young man when Jesus died in 33 A.D., perhaps as young as 18, would be a minimal age of 72 in 90A.D., the earliest possible date of the writing of the Gospel. If we go to the outside date, 110 A.D., John, if he was the author, would be 92, a ridiculously venerable age for this author. John begins his Gospel with the statement that used to be part of the Mass called "the Last Gospel." If the sermon had been longish the Last Gospel made it interminable, and if the Mass was going to be followed by Benediction, the Mass felt like a Good Friday three hour devotion. It was essentially a summation of Salvation History beginning with creation and ending with the Parousia. Secondly, it was the clearest statement of Trinitarian theology when compared to the other three canonic gospels. Thirdly, it is the most reactive to the Christian Persecutions by the Romans. In fact some scholars interpret John's 666 numbered beast as representative of the persecuting Roman emperors.

John told a very different story from the synoptic gospels, though in some ways it is closer to Mark, for like Mark, there are no infancy or childhood legends. Like Mark he cuts right to the chase. In fact, after his initial doxology he jumps right into the story of John the Baptist and his message of repentance and baptism. John presents the world in which Jesus' message of God's mercy is delivered, very similar to the Gospel of Mark, and yet the differences were significant.

What is remarkable are the encrustations of myths, legends and wishful thinking that essentially mask Jesus' potent message. What was that message and how was it skewed? That will be the subject of the next chapter.

The Message I Believe Jesus Preached

There are sequential documents that purport to be the record of the message of Jesus. The earliest recorded documents seem to be the two primary sources for what eventually became the four canonical gospels. The two sources are called *The Sayings of Jesus* and *The Quelle,* a German word that means source. These were accompanied by *The Passion Narrative.* It wasn't until somewhere between 65 and 75 A.D., during the attacks on Jerusalem by the Roman Army under the Emperor Vespasian and his sons Titus and Domitian that the canonical gospels were written.

During that period, the apostle Peter and the convert Paul had been executed in Rome under the Emperor Nero. The first apostle to be executed was James the Greater, frequently named the "brother" of the Lord, who was beheaded by a Roman sword in 44

A.D. When Mark's gospel was written the Christian movement was facing very dark days.

The principal lesson was that Jesus had announced the coming of a new kingdom. What exactly did he mean? Well, there have been ~~as~~ many varied interpretations of this proclamation. Some of Jesus' followers took a literal approach to the whole "Kingdom of God" thing. They actually thought that Jesus and his followers would be able to pull off a coup d'état, that his forces would overthrow the Jewish and Roman authorities and establish a civil government with true political power. Others, including the evangelists, presented Jesus' parables where they wrote "The Kingdom of God is like..." and then presented the story of the Good Samaritan, of the Owner of the Vineyard, or the Tale of the Talents, or the story where Jesus "suffers the little children." All of these evangelical stories indicate that Jesus' Proclamation of the Kingdom of God or the Kingdom of Heaven meant something completely different from a political kingdom or an earthly kingdom. Jesus' words in Mark are "The Kingdom of God is at hand, repent and believe the Good News (the Gospel)."

What exactly did he mean? What I believe is that the Kingdom of God, essentially the same thing said in the Lord's Prayer, ~~it~~ is a kingdom that happens inside the recipient. That is, once the converted believes the Good News he or she has a completely different perception. The externals don't change but the converted is able to see his or her life as invested in what he or she perceives as God's Will. Some translators interpret the word "repent" as "change your mind," align yourself with what you perceive as what God wants. So "the Kingdom of God is near" may mean that the higher the number of individuals who believe in this Kingdom, the necessary conversion to Jesus' message, that could result in a Kingdom of Heaven or God that would be realized.

I believe in something else. When we experience the change of hearts wherein we behave like the Good Samaritan or the Vinedresser etc., we begin to experience a spiritual Kingdom of Heaven.

Jesus had many other issues to present to his world. One of my favorites was his preaching of how forgiving God, his Father, really is. Over and over again he either preaches God's forgiveness in parables and in recorded events or demonstrates in his own forgiveness of sinners. The parable of the Prodigal Son presents an analog for God the Father in the person of the father of the prodigal son and his righteous brother. They both are jerks and their father forgives each of them for their sinfulness. In the story of the woman found in adultery, he turns the tables on the litigious Pharisees and asks, "Which of you will throw the first stone?" Seeing that her accusers have all disappeared He says to her, "Neither do I condemn you, go your way and sin no more."

Every time Jesus shows a forgiving heart, He is teaching that God's forgiveness is the same.

Beyond the Kingdom and Divine Mercy, Jesus pursued a policy of challenging the righteous Pharisees. Each time they challenged His adherence to the Mosaic Law and their own emendations Jesus questions their authority. When he is on trial for his life before Pontius Pilate, he calls Pilate's authority into question. This may be an evangelical interpolation. The evangelists were continually proving that Jesus was indeed God or the Second Person of the Blessed Trinity, God's only Son. But at no point in any of the three synoptic Gospels does he claim Deity though he frequently is shown to indicate that he is God's Son. Unfortunately, the fourth Gospel, the one written at least sixty years after Jesus' death and resurrection, has him continually claim sonship of God the Father. But there are many reasons to find this Gospel suspect because of its assertions.

Jesus as quoted in the synoptic Gospels described himself as the "Son of Man," not the "Son of God." And since this self-named "Son of Man," which some commentators say Jesus identified more with a human identity and by calling God his Father implying that we are also God's sons and daughters as he is Son of God.

In addition Jesus is shown to have little patience with the way in which the Israel of his day has been separated from the trust and faith in God which had governed Israel for so many centuries. When He drove the money lenders out of the Temple he was fed up with the way the religion of Israel had been corrupted by money and greed. Jesus had questioned the rulers and church leaders before His cleansing of the temple but it seems that this was the last straw for the religious and political leaders in Jerusalem.

When He says "I came to save the lost sheep of the House of Israel," he indicates that his mission is to the lost and confused and the despairing. In one of His most famous quotes He says, "It is easier for a camel to pass through the eye of a needle than for a rich man to enter the Kingdom of Heaven." He definitely is much more sympathetic to the poor and the downtrodden than to the wealthy and powerful. And finally when he preaches about the Last Judgment, one of the most fearsome things for sinful humans, he doesn't say, "I'll only save the perfect, those who have never sinned." He doesn't even mention sin, instead He says, "If you have fed and clothed and housed the poorest, if you have loved your poorest brothers with compassion, then you will be deserving of a place at my right side."

In the Lord's Prayer He exhorts us to "Forgive us our trespasses as we forgive those who trespass against us." Translation, if we would like forgiveness from God for our sinfulness we should be willing to extend the same forgiveness to those who have injured us.

There is a lot in the four Gospels that could be open to question as to if it ever actually happened or were some of these encrustations simply wishful thinking on the part of the evangelists and the communities to which they wrote desired to claim. And does it make a difference? Jesus' message was so powerful that it forced him to pay the ultimate price. He must have been tremendously threatening to the political and religious authorities of Israel and Rome to merit crucifixion. But perhaps the most compelling lesson of Jesus comes in his emphasis on Love. When a legalistic Pharisee asked Jesus "What is the greatest commandment?" Jesus responded with a quotation from the Jewish Prayer known as the Shema Yisrael: "You shall love the Lord your God with your whole heart and your whole mind and your whole might." He is quoting the prayer in Deuteronomy, and then he follows it with a quote from Leviticus 19:18 "Love your neighbor as yourself." But it is in John's Gospel where Love is showcased the most. Jesus says "God is Love," elevating it to the highest possible position in the Universe.

That pretty much summarizes the message of Jesus regarding the Kingdom, Forgiveness and Love. His message clearly indicated that active love of one's neighbor and one's enemies rather than righteous behavior was the key to salvation. Not only that, but he emphasizes the willingness to imitate Divine Forgiveness by forgiving those who wrong us.

So what happened to this beautiful and generous message?

How Jesus' Simple Message Was Corrupted

How did Jesus' simple Gospel become so convolutedly mangled?

Well, actually before the four canonical Gospels had been written, the Jewish persecutor of Christians, Saul of Tarsus, experienced his fall from a horse and his white light experience. He converted to Christianity and became perhaps the most zealous apostle of Jesus' message. Except he skewed it, he added his own prejudices and fears. If Jesus meant that his message was just for Jews, Paul at first just planned to go to the Jews of the Diaspora, those Jews who were still observant, but had moved to places in the Roman Empire but outside of the traditional boundaries of the Jewish Kingdom.

And unlike most of the other apostles, Paul wrote letters to the Christian Communities that he had founded. So we have very clear, unequivocal records of what Paul believed, taught and wrote.

One of the things that seems clear to me is that Paul's own history had forced him into a very judgmental position where he departs from Jesus' message of forgiveness to one of a greatly condemnatory position. Where Jesus forgives even the greatest sinners like Mary Magdalen, Paul has little tolerance for any kind of sexual sin. In my opinion it's a case of "you spot it, you got it." Instead of having compassion for sinners, especially sinners like him he has nothing but contempt for them. He writes the famous Epistle to the Romans where he produces Martin Luther's favorite line: "We are justified by faith," that is, as long as we believe we have attained salvation. Luther is famous for many things but perhaps the short hand expression "Pecca fortiter," in English "Sin on bravely." This in many ways appears to give comfort. In some ways it is in contradiction to the recorded words of Jesus who is said to have followed words of forgiveness with the words, "Go your way and sin no more."

But we must return to Paul. Although he is credited with carrying Jesus' message, first to the Jews of the diaspora and then extending this message to curious gentiles, which indeed got him the title of "Apostle of the Gentiles," it seems that his insistence on perfection blunted Jesus' message of forgiveness and the simple message of "the Kingdom of God is at hand," basically "Don't worry, God is in charge." Paul was so preoccupied with the tendency of his congregations to fall short of the mark that he comes across as a scold rather than a healer.

Then there's his fourth century follower, St. Augustine. Augustine of Hippo was a very troubled man. Famously, his mother, St. Monica, was constantly beset by her son's reckless and sinful youth. After a life of licentiousness in which he fathered an illegitimate son, Augustine experienced a conversion similar to St. Paul. While Paul went to Damascus to learn the teachings of Jesus, St. Augustine went to Milan and learned at the feet of St. Anselm, bishop of that northern Italian city. He eventually became Bishop of Hippo, a North African city very close to Carthage. He also became a prolific writer, his most famous books being *Confessions* and *The City of God.* The radical change in Augustine's lifestyle gives his writings a very guilty feel. The kind of judgment in which he engages seems to me far from the forgiving nature of Jesus' message and his recognition that humans are flawed. One might be curious to know how St. Paul would have viewed the parable of the Publican and the Pharisee. Jesus asked the question "Which of these two men was closer to God?" He implies that it is the sinful publican. Paul, on the other hand, was frequently critical of the sinful, in spite of his belief in the effectiveness of faith.

Then came Constantine. Between the death of Jesus and the Emperor Constantine's conversion to Christianity, the fellow members of his new religion had faced almost continuous persecution by the prior emperors' determination to use their armies to fight an uphill battle against the unstoppable burgeoning religion. As the barbarian hordes were nibbling at the northern borders of the Roman Empire while the Persians were posing a threat to the eastern borders, and the last thing Constantine needed in his army was a divisive religious question plaguing his soldiers. Whether he actually saw a cross in the heavens with the words "In hoc signo, vinces," in English, in this sign (the cross of Christ) may you conquer," or not, Constantine made a very big decision, one that had a history changing effect. He decided to convert to Christianity. The following year, 313 A.D., he issued the Edict of Milan, an edict that improved the treatment of Christians. Once he became a Christian and issued

71

an edict which almost made Christianity a most favored religion, practically making it not only tolerated but preferred, it wasn't long before it became the religion of the empire. However it was a religion more frequently practiced by the sophisticated residents of urban areas. Since the residents of rural areas were more conservative and had less contact with Christians they continued to practice the old Roman religion. The Latin word for the countryside is paganus, hence the religion practiced in the countryside is pagan, of the countryside. So the city folk chose to become Christians and decided to conform and join their neighbors who were becoming Christians, they saw which way the wind was blowing and that after being subjected to discrimination and martyrdom, they changed 180° and were now in the most favored group, or they were simply forced to convert. But the ministers of the state pretty much let those in countryside remain unChristianized, hence they gave their rural status the name of those who were labelled as religious pagans.

Once Constantine became a Christian and issued the Christianizing Edict of Milan, he then summoned the Council of Nicea in 325 A.D. in order to clarify exactly what being a Christian meant. That Council then authored the Nicene Creed stating clearly what Christians should believe. The most interesting thing about the 325 A.D. Nicene Creed was the lack of precision of the procession of the third person of the Blessed Trinity, the Holy Spirit. The clause simply states "We believe in the Holy Spirit. By the 381 revision the new creed states that the Holy Spirit proceeds from the God the Father; the words and the son or through the Son are nowhere to be found. The controversial term *filioque*, which means and the son, was added to the creed in Rome. This infuriated the orthodox Christians and has remained a point of division between Greek and Latin Christians to this day.

Before Constantine began to dabble in religious affairs by becoming a Christian, issuing an edict of toleration of Christianity, and summoning the first ecumenical council in order to clarify Christian belief there had been a great deal of controversy among the fledgling Christian communities. But once Constantine brought legitimacy, and as some historians say, brought Christianity under the imperial aegis, it was as though the floodgates had been unleashed. Heresies blossomed and controversies began to roil the church. Constantine and his successors attempted to referee the disputes that had preceded legitimacy. Once the creed was established, those who had other views began to make them well known. And those who opposed them quickly accused the others of heretical beliefs. There were those who completely denied the divinity of Jesus and those who were befuddled by the combination of Jesus' divinity and humanity. Some thought his humanity was an illusion. And some were more troubled about whether Mary was the mother of Jesus of the human half and not the mother of God. Pandora's Box had been opened and peace and harmony were nowhere in sight.

Eventually the Pope in Rome remained in charge in the West while the successors of Constantine held power of the church in the East with the Orthodox Patriarchs. The unity that Constantine had sought was lost forever.

Monasticism had its beginnings in the deserts of Egypt but gained its foothold in the West when St. Benedict wrote his rule for his followers and this became the source for the rest of the monastic communities in the West. The rigors and regularity of these monks had a profound effect on the rest of the church leadership. The first monk to be elected Pope was Gregory

I. He sent a fellow Benedictine, Augustine of Canterbury, to convert England. These monks brought all their vows with them and introduced lives of celibacy which eventually became the norm for the priestly life. In addition to restricting priestly life to the unmarried, the celibate, it established the assumption that priestly or monastic life was far superior to the more common married life. This created a hierarchy of religious classes. Those in religious life were considered far superior to those in lay life. This division presumed that everyone in religious life lived a life of perfection, by implication without sin. Therefore the possibility of sexual relations with anyone, especially homosexual relations frightened the daylights out of monastic authorities. Once the monastic popes started reigning they brought their anti-homosexual beliefs to the fore. After years of de-emphasizing the focus on homosexuality, it became obsession number one. Despite the fact that it was unwed heterosexuality, as best demonstrated by Rodrigo Borgia who became the serial father of half a dozen illegitimate children and reigned as Pope Alexander VI, the obsession with homosexuality would not go away. The Council of Trent brought an end to all sexual behavior by requiring celibacy for all men ordained priests.

This situation persisted into the 20th Century when the Gay Rights Movement really got underway.

The strident opposition to anything resembling equal rights for homosexuals by Popes John Paul II and Benedict XVI and their curial officials exacerbated the alienation of the Gay Community, so that the positions taken in the 11th Century by the monastic popes created even more resentment among a marginalized and desperate group. The AIDS epidemic had decimated this community and the purported compassion was invalidated by judgment and condemnation.

I will address the disastrous situation in which the Catholic Church finds itself in opposition to the basic welcoming and forgiving postures Jesus had taken, in the next chapter.

My Criticism of the Catholic Church's Mistakes How the Church's Positions Deviate from Jesus' Position

Where do I begin? It seems to me that the departures from the integrity of Jesus' teachings happened after his commission of the Apostles, after the Ascension/Resurrection event. The Bible tells us that following the departure of Jesus, the Apostles hid out in the "Upper Room," supposedly the place where the Last Supper occurred, until Pentecost when the Holy Spirit filled them with the courage and other virtues that would allow them to face a hostile audience and world and begin preaching Jesus' message of salvation and hope, they were petrified. Once they received that courage they were no longer fearful and began their mission of conversion. Since Jesus had said that his message was for the Jewish people, they were the first recipients of Jesus' message.

Paul, who was a Jew named Saul before his conversion, had been a righteous persecutor of the Jews who had become Christians. According to the Acts of the Apostles, Paul had a

tremendous fall from a horse, was
blinded and was challenged by the
voice of Jesus who asked Saul, "Why
dost thou persecute me?" Paul sought
instruction in the new Christian faith
and became what his title proclaims,
"The Apostle of the Gentiles." He
began by journeying to communities of
Jews of the diaspora in the Eastern
Roman Empire as far west as the city
of Rome itself. But in short order he
began to convert gentiles to the new
religion. He was so successful in his
gentile conversions that he created the
church's first divisive issue, the
circumcision of non-Jewish Christians.

Paul, however, was the first to move
away from the kind of acceptance of
all Jesus' message had preached. Jesus
had incredible compassion for the poor
and sinful. He always looked at them
with love and encouraged them to live
better lives. Paul was frequently
critical and rarely understanding or
forgiving. He seems to have been the
one to have created the paradigm for a

church that would expect perfection rather than understand that to be human means to be imperfect.

And it is more than likely that this outlook created the attitude, later fully embraced by the church at large, that only the perfect could be worthy of receiving the sacraments. This is probably the way that the church ended up deviating most from Jesus.

In the gospels Jesus is quoted as "having come to save the lost sheep of the house of Israel." How can you save anyone you deem as lost if you expect him to be perfect before you will save him? Jesus offered baptism, forgiveness, and Eucharist to those he knew to be sinners, but Paul and the church reversed this.

As the church grew following the missionary pilgrimages of Paul and the other Apostles, they simply adopted Paul's exclusiveness. Despite the fact that Jesus welcomed, embraced, ate meals and forgave sinners, Paul and his subsequent successors continued to make it more and more difficult for ordinary persons, particularly known sinners to have access to the healing sacraments. Does this sound crazy? Does it sound like they are not imitating Jesus? It does to me and it also continues to present a huge distance between the members of the church who were and are approved, and those who are not.

Recently, the current pope, who is credited with much more acceptance than his two predecessors, and is considered much more moderate than those same two predecessors, actually said that divorced Catholics will be welcome at Mass; they still may not receive the healing sacrament of Eucharist. Isn't that a lot like inviting someone to dinner at your home but then telling that person that there is not enough food for him to eat? How obnoxious, how disgusting, how unjust, it is almost impossible to countenance. Divorce is a heartbreaking thing. A family and two adults have their lives shattered. Even if both adults think divorce is the best thing for them, it is not going to remove the sting. If the cause of the divorce is the mistreatment of one of the spouses, divorce is probably the only path to safety. Should the wronged spouse be deprived of the sacraments because he or she has tried to make the best of a bad situation? And shouldn't there be a path of healing to get back to receiving the sacraments other than just saying, "No, you can't." Obviously the reasons for divorce are as diverse as those seeking them. Sometimes they are necessary to protect the endangered spouse. Living with an unpredictable chronic alcoholic or drug addicted person where there is little chance of reform and recovery seems to be a case in which the sober spouse needs to protect him or herself as well as any children born to this failed marriage. Should the person tortured in this marriage be deprived of grace and health giving sacraments like Eucharist? Isn't this beyond belief cruelty?

Obviously, it has taken a long time for society to recognize that a significant portion of society is homosexual through no fault of their own. World and American psychiatrists and psychologists have recognized that being attracted to persons of the same sex is as natural for homosexuals as being attracted to persons of the opposite sex is for heterosexuals. Why is the Church so unwilling to accept this advance in the understanding of homosexual orientation and behavior? Gay Catholics need guidance, forgiveness and the sacraments just as much as heterosexual Catholics. Why is this so difficult for the Church? Tradition and prejudice have prevented understanding in my opinion. Lives have been destroyed and lost due to this intransigence. Just as divorced

Catholics need the solace the Church is able to offer, so do homosexual Catholics. What is really necessary is a deeper understanding of human sexuality from persons who are not bound by celibacy. The current approach is not working.

There is also something grotesquely wrong with the way that children are taught about how God figures in their lives and the way that adults continue to grow through intelligent adult homilies. But the current crop of homilists, at least in the USA, are so afraid of being delated to the Holy See, that they avoid any statement that might be misconstrued. By the way, perhaps you are unfamiliar with the verb delate. With regard to homilists who take risks in their homilies the word delate means to report anonymously something one either does not like or approve or understand to the Holy See in order to cast a negative light on the disapproved homilist. This has placed such a damper on delving into the real meanings of scriptural passages. Instead they play it safe and preach to adults as though they are as ignorant as little children. For intelligent, questioning and educated adult Catholics there is nothing or nonsense.

Having mentioned children I need to discuss the way children are educated in the Catholic faith. The confusion that runs throughout the Old and New Testament is never explained. Children are taught that it is necessary to love God, but what that actually means is never explained, instead of explaining the reasons why one should want to love God and how one actually does that. I know I was never taught, and I went to 16 years of Catholic schools. The Hebrew command quoted by Jesus is very clear. "You shall love the Lord your God with your whole heart and your whole soul and your whole mind." But no one goes to the trouble of explaining this or describing how. One has to figure out

how to do this but ~~giving~~ given no idea how
or why. This is a problem.

Let's look at another huge problem
facing the Church since the time of
Constantine. Instead of having a
clergy and a hierarchy that truly are the
servants of the servants of God, the
clergy have been elevated to a special
place and they are perceived by
themselves and their congregations as
indeed better than the men and women
in the pews. But when a pervasive
pedophile scandal is uncovered and the
hierarchy's collusion in the cover-up
of the pervasive scandal gives the lie to
the idea that Churchmen are a cut
above the ordinary folks in the pews
drives well intentioned Catholics out
of the pews. The fact that this problem
has had lip-service paid, but the
response has been less than thorough is
a huge problem. The fact that instead
of requiring Bernard Cardinal Law to
stay in Boston to face the
consequences for his negligence with
regard to the exploding priestly

pedophile scandal Pope John Paull II, is such a heinous and egregious act it seems perfect grounds to insist on rescinding his cause for canonization and his sainthood.

I don't know if this is a problem in the rest of the world but it has been a significant problem in the United States. The problem is the appointment of bishopsand archbishops. These particular issues do not stem from the deviation from the customs that Jesus supposedly established. ~~No~~ this is a custom that began in cities like Rome, Antioch and Alexandria, is church related not Christ related. Originally local churches elected their bishops from the local clergy. Even the first Catholic bishop in the United States, John Carroll, first bishop of Baltimore, was a native of Baltimore. John Carroll was a Jesuit professor at Georgetown until the Jesuits were suppressed in 1773 by the Pope. He became a secular priest and then was consecrated bishop in 1789 beginning his episcopate as George Washington began his presidency. John Carroll should have been the model for episcopal selection. The practice of election had been replaced with papal appointment but for many years the practice was to send a terna, a list of three men deemed worthy of the episcopate by the clergy of the diocese. The group was in the diocese choosing three qualified men of the diocese. As the position of bishop became more tinged by politics it frequently happened that a diocese did not have a political "buddy" in the diocese, instead someone deemed acceptable by the pope no matter how little he knew about the diocese. This is a tremendously bad for the diocese and for the church.

Probably one of the severest problems in the church today is facing is the declining number of clergy. The huge seminary classes that were ordained after World War II to the post Vatican

II upheaval are gone. Several years ago the largest archdiocese in the United States ordained four men to fill the places being left by the large number of men who have served long after a typical retirement age of 65 and are now so old that they can't do much more than celebrate the occasional parish mass. This is an unsustainable path. Some of the solutions are married clergy or the ordination of women. These are interesting solutions but may be too extreme for the faithful. But then faithful are disappearing as quickly as clergy. This is really the central "Titanic" issue. If the church is disappearing, what difference does personnel crisis matter? One possible solution is to create a new form of weekend priests whose only function is to celebrate masses on Sunday and live ordinary lives as married men on weekdays, sort of like the permanent diaconate.

Another glaring problem is the status of women in the church, which currently is less than second class, more like nothing. Because of their status being so miniscule the church has been ignoring them since shortly after the apostolic period when the order of female deacons was suppressed. There is chatter that this order may be revived. That would definitely be a start and could allow women to be appointed cardinals and be electors for the pope. I personally am opposed to the ordination of women to the priesthood because of their unique office as stand-ins for Jesus, who lived among us as a male. But I think ordaining them to the deaconate allows bringing a female perspective in electing the head of the Catholic Church. Currently all persons given a cardinal's hat must be ordained priests. Changing that rule and nomination to the College of Cardinals would be the equivalent of the 19th Amendment that gave American women the right to vote. It would be very interesting; I wonder what the chances of this happening are.

The church has many problems today, but I think the most significant is the constant attrition. Today what is happening is that more and more Catholics who have not actually left the church, the so-called Recovering Catholics or just ex-Catholics, are still nominally Catholic and want to be baptized, married and buried but otherwise participation is horribly lax. There are those referred to as "C&E Catholics." These folks are little more involved but their label refers to their peculiar attendance and participation on C & E, that is Christmas and Easter, they might even say to themselves, "We should try and attend mass more frequently," but they don't. There are those who don't attend at all, but they love the current pope.

I suppose Catholics like the above mentioned are enumerated with the rest. The pews don't uphold these numbers. They are frequently bordering on empty. As the Second

Vatican Council relaxed so many traditional rules which used to separate practicing Catholics from other Christians, the willingness to make sure one kept the Sundays and Holy Days with Mass attendance and abided by the church regulations regarding fast and abstinence have been more honored in the breach than in the actual observance. There was a law of the church regarding Catholics marrying non-Catholics, whereby all children born of these marriages had to be raised in the Catholic faith. This law seems to be totally disregarded today. What it means to be a Catholic today is much more confusing than it used to be. When the Pope Paul VI refused to bring the church up to date with regard to birth control he signaled the mass disobedience by Catholic women in economically progressive countries. That was followed by the mass exodus from the pews and the pitiful financial support these erstwhile Catholics are willing to make.

I insist that the biggest problem for Catholic church is their illingness to address the transition trom being a child Catholic to being an adult Catholic. Instead of holding adult education classes to inform Catholics of advances being made in the understanding of the formation of the Bible stories,and that more and more of them are legends and allegories rather than fact,leaves adults wondering why they were told what essentially are lies rather than dogmatic truth leaves adult Catholics wondering what they can believe or are expected to believe.

I am very concerned about what is going to happen to the church in the coming centuries. It has lost most of the educated world who wonder at this relic encrusted with jewels which becomes more and more irrelevant in the lives of the world. We applaud their good works, abhor their gigantic sins and wonder how long this *Titanic* can stay afloat.

I started the second section of this book discussing some of the lessons I had learned from the book *Who Wrote the Bible?* Aside from learning that the first five books of the Hebrew Testament, what Christians call the Old Testament and Jews call *Torah* has traditionally been considered the literary output of the great leader Moses. But the book previously mentioned purports to prove that the first five books and several after that were written before and after the Babylonian captivity, that each of the four authors had very different perspectives and were very different in their opinions of the relations of humans with God, in which one side views God from a very authoritarian judgmental and distant God and one that sees God from a very loving and forgiving perspective. According to one source God is always disapproving and distant. According to the other God is close to us, loves us and is amazingly forgiving. This

97

schizophrenic God has been a source of great consternation and confusion. No wonder the Catholic Church has had such a difficult time wrestling with God's perceived schizophrenia.

How the Catholic Church has failed me and so many other Catholics

In this final chapter I have to summarize my conclusions of how the Catholic Church has failed in its mission to carry Jesus' simple message of love and forgiveness. There have been so many distractions that have driven church authorities, particularly the main leadership positions, which this is difficult to explain. More often than not it is the seven deadly sins that have derailed them.

Pride has forced popes, cardinals and bishops to make self-serving choices that condemned or harmed the faithful and their enemies while protecting their own positions. Fighting and dividing with Luther instead of recognizing his calls for reform immediately comes to mind.

Anger has been displayed so many times in the church's punitive behavior toward the questioning and those having trouble understanding irrational or suspect teaching. Galileo and

Cervantes seem to be the first in my thoughts.

Lust, this sin seems to have been the most frequent causing problems to the church. Early monasticism chose celibacy and chastity for clergy as a form of penance equivalent to fasting. Just like diabetics who were constantly advised to avoid sweets and thus became obsessed with candy, much to their ruin, so dividing religious behavior from sexuality which caused papal bastards, cardinal nephews, and pedophile priests.

Sloth, this sin was exemplified by the behavior of Pope Leo X with regard to Luther's initial legitimate protests and to the laziness of Pope Paul VI with regard to contraception. But perhaps the worst example of the sloth epidemic is the dreadful level of the sermons that are being delivered because of fear.

Gluttony is most obvious in the
tremendous alcoholism that has
plagued the clergy, most often as a
way to finesse celibacy and chastity.
Drinking oneself into oblivion may
prevent sexual activity; on the other
hand it may also contribute to sexual
license.

Greed frequently may be manifested
in ambition to be agreeable to be
promoted and enjoy privileges and
perquisites available from the church
and from wealthy parishioners,
including things like luxury
automobiles for special priests.

Envy, this most basic of human
frailties is just as common in the
church as well as outside it.

So the path to returning the church to
the virtues it exemplified in apostolic
times appears to be redeemable by
reverting to virtue rather than sin.
How easy do you think that will be?